EMMANUEL JOSEPH

Visionary Tactics, Comparing the Minds of Tech Moguls and Real Estate Tycoons

Copyright © 2025 by Emmanuel Joseph

All rights reserved. No part of this publication may be reproduced, stored or transmitted in any form or by any means, electronic, mechanical, photocopying, recording, scanning, or otherwise without written permission from the publisher. It is illegal to copy this book, post it to a website, or distribute it by any other means without permission.

First edition

This book was professionally typeset on Reedsy. Find out more at reedsy.com

Contents

1	Chapter 1: The Dawn of Two Empires	1
2	Chapter 2: Building Blocks of Innovation	3
3	Chapter 3: Strategic Vision and Leadership	5
4	Chapter 4: Financial Acumen and Investment Strategies	7
5	Chapter 4: Financial Acumen and Investment Strategies...	9
6	Chapter 5: Navigating Market Dynamics	10
7	Chapter 6: Risk Management and Resilience	12
8	Chapter 7: Branding and Public Perception	14
9	Chapter 8: Philanthropy and Social Responsibility	16
10	Chapter 9: Global Influence and Expansion	18
11	Chapter 10: Legacy and Succession Planning	20
12	Chapter 11: The Future of Tech and Real Estate	22
13	Chapter 11: The Future of Tech and Real Estate (continued)	23
14	Chapter 12: Lessons from Visionary Leaders	25

1

Chapter 1: The Dawn of Two Empires

The rise of technology and real estate empires has significantly shaped the landscape of modern commerce. Tech moguls, often seen as the architects of our digital future, have revolutionized how we communicate, work, and live. Their vision extends far beyond the confines of physical boundaries, tapping into the limitless potential of the digital world. In contrast, real estate tycoons have built their empires on tangible assets, transforming skylines and redefining urban living. Both realms, though vastly different, share a common thread: the relentless pursuit of innovation and growth.

The early days of tech moguls were marked by bold ideas and relentless experimentation. Pioneers like Steve Jobs and Bill Gates did not just build companies; they created ecosystems that continue to thrive and evolve. Their journeys were not without obstacles, but their ability to anticipate market needs and push the boundaries of technology set them apart. On the other side, real estate tycoons like Donald Trump and Sam Zell navigated a world of bricks and mortar. Their successes were built on strategic investments, market analysis, and an unyielding belief in the potential of prime real estate.

In the tech world, the focus is often on disruption. Visionaries like Elon Musk have redefined industries, from electric vehicles to space travel, by challenging conventional wisdom and embracing risk. In real estate, the approach is more about evolution and adaptation. Tycoons like Harry

VISIONARY TACTICS, COMPARING THE MINDS OF TECH MOGULS AND REAL ESTATE TYCOONS

Helmsley have shown that success lies in understanding market dynamics, recognizing opportunities for redevelopment, and executing ambitious projects that stand the test of time. Both paths require a keen sense of foresight and the ability to seize opportunities.

As these empires grew, their leaders became symbols of innovation and success. Tech moguls like Mark Zuckerberg, whose creation of Facebook reshaped social interaction, epitomize the impact of digital transformation. In real estate, figures like Leona Helmsley, known for her luxury hotel empire, represent the pinnacle of property development. Despite their different domains, the visionary tactics employed by these leaders share striking similarities in their strategic thinking and execution.

In this book, we delve into the minds of these visionary leaders, comparing their strategies, successes, and the lessons they offer for aspiring entrepreneurs. By exploring the parallels and divergences between tech moguls and real estate tycoons, we aim to uncover the underlying principles that drive their success and inspire the next generation of innovators.

2

Chapter 2: Building Blocks of Innovation

Innovation is the cornerstone of success for both tech moguls and real estate tycoons. For tech leaders, innovation often means creating something entirely new or disrupting an existing market. Companies like Apple and Microsoft didn't just introduce new products; they fundamentally changed the way people interact with technology. The drive to innovate is fueled by a desire to solve problems, improve user experiences, and stay ahead of the competition. This relentless pursuit of innovation is a defining characteristic of tech moguls.

In the real estate world, innovation manifests differently. It involves transforming underutilized spaces into vibrant communities, repurposing old buildings, and finding new ways to maximize property value. Real estate tycoons like Gerald Hines have been pioneers in this field, known for their ability to see potential where others see obstacles. Their innovation lies in their vision to create iconic structures that not only meet market demands but also stand as landmarks of architectural excellence.

Both tech and real estate leaders understand that innovation is not without its risks. In the tech industry, the rapid pace of change means that today's breakthrough can quickly become obsolete. Companies must continuously evolve, investing in research and development to stay relevant. This is exemplified by Google's constant experimentation with new products and services, even as they maintain their dominance in search and advertising.

In real estate, the risks are equally significant, with market fluctuations and economic downturns posing constant challenges. Successful tycoons mitigate these risks through diversification and strategic planning.

Collaboration is another key aspect of innovation. Tech moguls often foster a culture of collaboration within their organizations, encouraging cross-functional teams to work together on groundbreaking projects. This collaborative approach not only fosters creativity but also accelerates the development process. In real estate, collaboration often involves partnering with architects, urban planners, and local governments to bring ambitious projects to life. These partnerships are crucial in navigating regulatory hurdles and ensuring that developments are both commercially viable and socially responsible.

Ultimately, innovation is about anticipating future trends and staying ahead of the curve. For tech moguls, this means keeping an eye on emerging technologies and consumer behaviors. In real estate, it involves understanding demographic shifts, urbanization patterns, and environmental sustainability. Both industries require a forward-thinking mindset and the ability to adapt to changing circumstances. By embracing innovation, tech moguls and real estate tycoons alike have managed to build empires that continue to thrive in an ever-evolving world.

3

Chapter 3: Strategic Vision and Leadership

The success of tech moguls and real estate tycoons can be largely attributed to their strategic vision and leadership. Tech leaders like Jeff Bezos of Amazon and Larry Page of Google are known for their ability to envision the future and make bold decisions that shape the trajectory of their companies. Their leadership style is often characterized by a willingness to take calculated risks and a focus on long-term goals rather than short-term gains. This strategic vision is what sets them apart and allows them to navigate the rapidly changing tech landscape.

In real estate, strategic vision is equally important. Tycoons like Stephen Ross, founder of Related Companies, have built their empires by identifying and capitalizing on emerging trends in urban development. Their leadership involves a deep understanding of market dynamics, meticulous planning, and the ability to execute complex projects. Successful real estate leaders are not just developers; they are also visionary planners who can foresee the needs of future generations and create spaces that meet those needs.

Effective leadership in both industries involves the ability to inspire and motivate teams. Tech moguls often cultivate a culture of innovation and excellence within their organizations. They empower employees to think creatively, take initiative, and contribute to the company's vision. This approach not only drives innovation but also fosters a sense of ownership and commitment among employees. Similarly, real estate tycoons lead by example, demonstrating a strong work ethic and a commitment to quality. They build teams of skilled professionals who share their vision and work collaboratively to achieve ambitious goals.

Another critical aspect of leadership is the ability to adapt to changing circumstances. In the tech industry, where the pace of change is relentless, leaders must be agile and responsive. They need to be able to pivot quickly when new opportunities arise or when market conditions shift. This adaptability is exemplified by companies like Netflix, which transformed from a DVD rental service into a global streaming giant. In real estate, adaptability means being able to navigate economic cycles, regulatory changes, and evolving consumer preferences. Successful tycoons are those who can anticipate these changes and adjust their strategies accordingly.

Finally, ethical leadership is essential for long-term success. Tech moguls and real estate tycoons have a significant impact on society, and their decisions can shape the future of communities and industries. Ethical leadership involves making decisions that are not only profitable but also socially responsible. This includes considerations of sustainability, diversity, and community impact. Leaders like Elon Musk, who advocate for renewable energy and sustainable practices, set an example for others to follow. By prioritizing ethical considerations, tech moguls and real estate tycoons can build lasting legacies that benefit both their companies and society as a whole.

4

Chapter 4: Financial Acumen and Investment Strategies

Financial acumen is a critical component of success for both tech moguls and real estate tycoons. In the tech industry, financial expertise involves managing large-scale investments in research and development, navigating funding rounds, and strategically allocating resources to fuel growth. Leaders like Peter Thiel and Reid Hoffman are known for their ability to identify lucrative opportunities and make sound investment decisions that drive their companies forward. Their financial strategies are often characterized by a willingness to invest heavily in innovative ideas and the ability to attract and manage venture capital.

In real estate, financial acumen is equally important. Tycoons like Richard LeFrak and Sheldon Solow have built their fortunes through strategic investments in prime properties and savvy financial management. Their success is often attributed to their ability to identify undervalued assets, secure favorable financing, and execute profitable transactions. Real estate tycoons must also navigate complex financial landscapes, including market fluctuations, interest rate changes, and economic cycles. Their financial strategies involve meticulous planning, risk management, and the ability to adapt to changing market conditions.

Both tech moguls and real estate tycoons understand the importance of diversification in their investment strategies. In the tech industry, diversification involves investing in a broad range of technologies and business models to mitigate risk. Companies like Alphabet, the parent company of Google, have diversified their portfolios to include ventures in artificial intelligence, autonomous vehicles, and healthcare. This approach not only spreads risk but also opens up new revenue streams and growth opportunities. In real estate, diversification involves investing in different types of properties, such as residential, commercial, and industrial, as well as exploring new markets and geographic regions. Tycoons who diversify their portfolios can weather economic downturns and capitalize on emerging trends.

Another key aspect of financial acumen is the ability to leverage debt and equity to fuel growth. Tech moguls often rely on venture capital and public offerings to raise funds for expansion and innovation. They must strike a balance between maintaining control of their companies and securing the necessary capital to achieve their goals. In real estate, leveraging debt through mortgages and other financing instruments is a common practice. Tycoons who skillfully manage debt can acquire valuable properties and execute large-scale developments without overextending their resources.

Ultimately, financial acumen involves making informed decisions based on thorough analysis and a deep understanding of market dynamics. Both tech moguls and real estate tycoons rely on data and insights to guide their investment strategies. They use financial models, market research, and predictive analytics to
   continue

5

Chapter 4: Financial Acumen and Investment Strategies (continued)

guide their decisions and anticipate future trends. By combining financial acumen with visionary leadership, tech moguls and real estate tycoons have built enduring legacies that continue to influence their respective industries.

6

Chapter 5: Navigating Market Dynamics

Understanding and navigating market dynamics is crucial for both tech moguls and real estate tycoons. In the tech industry, market dynamics are influenced by factors such as technological advancements, consumer preferences, and competitive pressures. Leaders like Satya Nadella of Microsoft have shown the ability to adapt to changing market conditions and capitalize on emerging opportunities. Their success lies in their ability to read market signals, pivot when necessary, and maintain a competitive edge through continuous innovation.

In real estate, market dynamics are shaped by economic conditions, demographic trends, and regulatory changes. Tycoons like Stephen Ross have demonstrated a keen understanding of these factors and have successfully navigated the complexities of the real estate market. Their ability to anticipate market shifts and make strategic investments has been key to their success. Real estate leaders must also be adept at managing risks, such as market downturns and regulatory challenges, to protect their investments and ensure long-term profitability.

Both tech moguls and real estate tycoons rely on data and analytics to inform their decisions. In the tech industry, companies use big data and artificial intelligence to gain insights into consumer behavior, optimize operations, and develop new products. This data-driven approach allows tech leaders to make informed decisions and stay ahead of the competition. In real

CHAPTER 5: NAVIGATING MARKET DYNAMICS

estate, data analytics is used to assess market conditions, evaluate property values, and identify investment opportunities. Tycoons who leverage data and analytics can make more informed decisions and maximize their returns.

Adaptability is another critical aspect of navigating market dynamics. Tech moguls must be able to respond to rapidly changing technology trends and evolving consumer demands. Companies like Amazon have thrived by continuously innovating and expanding their product offerings to meet market needs. In real estate, adaptability means being able to respond to shifts in demand, such as the rise of remote work and the increased demand for flexible office spaces. Real estate leaders who can anticipate and respond to these changes are better positioned to succeed in a dynamic market environment.

Finally, strategic partnerships play a vital role in navigating market dynamics. Tech moguls often collaborate with other companies, research institutions, and startups to drive innovation and expand their market presence. These partnerships enable tech leaders to access new technologies, tap into new markets, and accelerate their growth. In real estate, partnerships with architects, urban planners, and local governments are essential for executing large-scale projects and navigating regulatory challenges. By building strong partnerships, real estate tycoons can enhance their ability to deliver successful projects and create value for their stakeholders.

Chapter 6: Risk Management and Resilience

Risk management is a fundamental aspect of success for both tech moguls and real estate tycoons. In the tech industry, risks come in many forms, including cybersecurity threats, regulatory challenges, and market volatility. Leaders like Tim Cook of Apple have demonstrated the ability to manage these risks through robust security measures, compliance with regulations, and strategic planning. Effective risk management involves identifying potential threats, assessing their impact, and implementing strategies to mitigate them.

In real estate, risks are often related to economic cycles, market fluctuations, and regulatory changes. Tycoons like Sam Zell have built their empires by carefully managing these risks and making strategic decisions to protect their investments. This includes diversifying their portfolios, securing long-term financing, and maintaining flexibility in their development plans. Successful real estate leaders are also adept at managing operational risks, such as construction delays and cost overruns, to ensure that projects are completed on time and within budget.

Resilience is another key aspect of risk management. Tech moguls and real estate tycoons must be able to weather setbacks and bounce back from challenges. In the tech industry, resilience involves the ability to adapt

CHAPTER 6: RISK MANAGEMENT AND RESILIENCE

to changing market conditions, recover from failures, and continuously innovate. Companies like Twitter have shown resilience by pivoting their business models and finding new ways to engage users and generate revenue. In real estate, resilience means being able to withstand economic downturns, adjust to changing market demands, and execute projects in the face of adversity. Tycoons who demonstrate resilience can navigate challenges and emerge stronger.

Both industries require a proactive approach to risk management and resilience. This involves continuous monitoring of potential risks, developing contingency plans, and fostering a culture of adaptability and innovation. By staying ahead of potential threats and building resilient organizations, tech moguls and real estate tycoons can protect their investments and achieve long-term success.

In this book, we explore the visionary tactics that have driven the success of tech moguls and real estate tycoons. By comparing their strategies, leadership styles, and approaches to innovation, we aim to uncover the principles that can inspire and guide the next generation of entrepreneurs. Through their stories, we gain insights into the mindset and tactics that have shaped the modern business landscape and continue to drive progress in the digital age and the built environment.

8

Chapter 7: Branding and Public Perception

The power of branding and public perception cannot be underestimated in the success of tech moguls and real estate tycoons. For tech leaders, establishing a strong brand is essential in building trust with consumers and differentiating their products in a competitive market. Iconic brands like Apple and Tesla have created loyal customer bases through a combination of innovative products, compelling storytelling, and a consistent brand image. Leaders like Steve Jobs and Elon Musk have used their personal brands to amplify the visibility and appeal of their companies, often becoming synonymous with their brand's identity.

In the real estate industry, branding is equally important. Tycoons like Harry Macklowe and Donald Bren have built prestigious brands that are associated with luxury, quality, and innovation. Successful real estate developers understand that a strong brand can increase property values, attract high-quality tenants, and create a sense of prestige and desirability around their projects. They invest in marketing, public relations, and community engagement to build a positive perception of their developments and establish a lasting legacy.

Public perception is shaped not only by branding but also by the leaders' actions and reputations. Tech moguls who are seen as visionary, innovative, and socially responsible can enhance their brand's credibility and attract talent, investors, and customers. Leaders like Bill Gates, who have focused on philanthropy and social impact, have strengthened their personal and corporate brands by demonstrating a commitment to making a positive difference in the world. In real estate, tycoons who prioritize sustainability, community development, and ethical business practices can build a positive reputation and create long-term value for their stakeholders.

Media plays a significant role in shaping public perception. Tech moguls and real estate tycoons who effectively leverage media coverage can amplify their influence and reach. This includes traditional media channels such as newspapers, television, and magazines, as well as digital platforms like social media, blogs, and podcasts. By sharing their vision, achievements, and thought leadership through various media channels, leaders can build a strong public presence and connect with a broader audience.

Finally, transparency and authenticity are critical in building and maintaining a positive public perception. Tech moguls and real estate tycoons who communicate openly and honestly with their stakeholders can build trust and credibility. This involves being transparent about business practices, financial performance, and future plans, as well as acknowledging and addressing any challenges or controversies. Authentic leaders who stay true to their values and principles are more likely to resonate with their audience and create a lasting positive impact.

9

Chapter 8: Philanthropy and Social Responsibility

P hilanthropy and social responsibility are integral to the legacies of many tech moguls and real estate tycoons. These leaders recognize that their success comes with a responsibility to give back to society and address pressing social and environmental issues. Tech moguls like Bill and Melinda Gates have made significant contributions through their foundation, focusing on global health, education, and poverty alleviation. Their philanthropic efforts have not only made a tangible impact on millions of lives but have also set an example for other leaders to follow.

In the real estate industry, tycoons like Eli Broad and John Arrillaga have made substantial philanthropic contributions to education, arts, and community development. Real estate leaders often focus on initiatives that improve the quality of life in the communities where they operate. This includes funding affordable housing projects, supporting local schools and cultural institutions, and investing in infrastructure improvements. By aligning their philanthropic efforts with their business goals, real estate tycoons can create a positive social impact while enhancing the value of their developments.

Corporate social responsibility (CSR) is another key aspect of giving back. Tech companies like Google and Microsoft have implemented comprehensive

CSR programs that address environmental sustainability, diversity and inclusion, and ethical business practices. These programs not only benefit society but also contribute to the company's reputation and employee satisfaction. Real estate companies that prioritize sustainability in their developments, such as green building practices and energy-efficient designs, demonstrate a commitment to environmental stewardship and attract socially conscious tenants and investors.

Both tech moguls and real estate tycoons understand that philanthropy and social responsibility are long-term investments. By contributing to the well-being of society and the environment, they create a more sustainable and equitable future for all. Their philanthropic initiatives also serve as a source of inspiration and motivation for their employees, stakeholders, and the broader community. Ultimately, the impact of their generosity extends far beyond financial contributions, influencing social norms, shaping public policies, and driving positive change.

In this chapter, we explore the diverse ways in which tech moguls and real estate tycoons engage in philanthropy and social responsibility. By examining their motivations, strategies, and outcomes, we gain insights into the principles that guide their efforts and the lessons they offer for future leaders. Through their stories, we see the profound difference that visionary leaders can make in addressing some of the world's most pressing challenges.

10

Chapter 9: Global Influence and Expansion

The influence of tech moguls and real estate tycoons extends far beyond their home markets. Both industries have seen significant global expansion, driven by the vision and ambition of their leaders. Tech companies like Amazon, Google, and Facebook have established a strong global presence, with operations and customers in virtually every corner of the world. This expansion is fueled by the scalability of digital technologies, the global nature of the internet, and the ability to adapt products and services to diverse markets.

Real estate tycoons have also ventured into international markets, capitalizing on opportunities in emerging economies and established global cities. Leaders like Gerald Hines have successfully developed projects in Europe, Asia, and the Middle East, bringing their expertise in high-quality developments to new markets. Global expansion in real estate involves navigating diverse regulatory environments, understanding local market dynamics, and building partnerships with local stakeholders. Successful tycoons leverage their experience and networks to execute projects that meet the unique demands of each market.

Both tech moguls and real estate tycoons understand the importance of cultural sensitivity and adaptability in their global operations. In the tech

CHAPTER 9: GLOBAL INFLUENCE AND EXPANSION

industry, companies must tailor their products and marketing strategies to resonate with local cultures and preferences. This includes offering localized content, language support, and region-specific features. In real estate, cultural considerations influence design choices, community engagement, and business practices. Tycoons who respect and integrate local customs and values into their developments are more likely to succeed in international markets.

Global influence also comes with responsibilities. Tech moguls and real estate tycoons have the power to shape economic development, urbanization, and technological innovation on a global scale. Their decisions can impact job creation, infrastructure development, and access to technology and housing. As global leaders, they must consider the broader implications of their actions and contribute to sustainable and inclusive growth. This includes addressing issues such as digital inequality, affordable housing, and environmental sustainability.

In this chapter, we explore the strategies and challenges of global expansion for tech moguls and real estate tycoons. By examining their successes and lessons learned, we gain insights into the principles that guide their international ventures. Through their stories, we see how visionary leaders can create a positive impact on a global scale, driving progress and innovation across diverse markets.

11

Chapter 10: Legacy and Succession Planning

The legacy of tech moguls and real estate tycoons is shaped not only by their achievements but also by their ability to plan for the future. Succession planning is a critical aspect of ensuring the continuity and longevity of their empires. Tech leaders like Bill Gates and Larry Page have carefully planned their transitions, appointing successors who share their vision and values. Effective succession planning involves identifying and grooming future leaders, establishing clear leadership structures, and ensuring a smooth transition of power.

In the real estate industry, succession planning is equally important. Tycoons like Larry Silverstein have focused on passing their knowledge and expertise to the next generation, ensuring that their companies continue to thrive. This involves mentoring and developing future leaders, creating a strong organizational culture, and setting long-term strategic goals. Successful real estate tycoons understand that their legacy is not just about their individual achievements but also about the lasting impact of their work on the industry and the communities they serve.

Both tech moguls and real estate tycoons recognize the importance of preserving their values and vision in their succession plans. This includes maintaining a commitment to innovation, quality, and social responsibility.

CHAPTER 10: LEGACY AND SUCCESSION PLANNING

By instilling these principles in their successors, leaders can ensure that their companies continue to operate with the same level of excellence and integrity. Clear communication and transparency are essential in this process, as they help build trust and alignment within the organization.

Another critical aspect of legacy planning is philanthropy. Many tech moguls and real estate tycoons have established foundations and charitable trusts to continue their philanthropic efforts beyond their lifetimes. These initiatives are designed to address long-term social and environmental challenges, create opportunities for future generations, and uphold the leaders' commitment to giving back. By creating enduring philanthropic legacies, tech moguls and real estate tycoons can make a lasting positive impact on society.

In this chapter, we explore the principles and practices of legacy and succession planning for tech moguls and real estate tycoons. By examining their approaches to leadership transition, mentoring, and philanthropy, we gain insights into the strategies that ensure the continuity and lasting impact of their work. Through their stories, we see how visionary leaders can build enduring legacies that inspire and guide future generations.

12

Chapter 11: The Future of Tech and Real Estate

As we look to the future, the paths of tech moguls and real estate tycoons are likely to continue evolving in response to emerging trends and challenges. The tech industry is poised for significant advancements in areas such as artificial intelligence, quantum computing, and biotechnology. Visionary leaders like Sundar Pichai and Satya Nadella are already positioning their companies to capitalize on these innovations, driving progress and shaping the future of technology. The integration of technology into everyday life will continue to transform industries, enhance productivity, and improve quality of life.

13

Chapter 11: The Future of Tech and Real Estate (continued)

In real estate, the future is shaped by trends such as urbanization, sustainability, and the rise of smart cities. Visionary leaders like Frank Gehry and Jonathan Goldstein are already exploring innovative solutions to address these challenges. Urbanization continues to drive demand for housing and commercial spaces, leading to the development of mixed-use projects and transit-oriented developments. Sustainability is becoming a key focus, with an emphasis on green building practices, renewable energy, and environmentally friendly materials. The integration of technology into real estate, through smart buildings and IoT (Internet of Things) devices, is also transforming the way we live and work.

The convergence of technology and real estate is likely to create new opportunities and challenges for both industries. Smart cities, which use data and technology to enhance urban living, are becoming a reality in many parts of the world. These cities leverage sensors, connectivity, and data analytics to improve infrastructure, transportation, and public services. Tech moguls and real estate tycoons are collaborating to develop smart city projects that offer innovative solutions to urban challenges and create more sustainable, efficient, and livable environments.

As we move forward, the role of technology in shaping the built environment will continue to grow. Tech moguls and real estate tycoons who embrace this convergence and explore new ways to integrate technology into their projects will be well-positioned to lead the future. This includes leveraging technologies such as virtual reality, augmented reality, and artificial intelligence to enhance design, construction, and property management. The future of tech and real estate is interconnected, and visionary leaders who recognize and harness this synergy will drive progress and create lasting impact.

In this chapter, we explore the emerging trends and innovations that will shape the future of tech and real estate. By examining the opportunities and challenges ahead, we gain insights into the strategies that will drive success in an evolving landscape. Through the stories of visionary leaders, we see how the convergence of technology and real estate can create a more sustainable, efficient, and connected world.

14

Chapter 12: Lessons from Visionary Leaders

The journeys of tech moguls and real estate tycoons offer valuable lessons for aspiring entrepreneurs and leaders. Their stories are a testament to the power of vision, innovation, and resilience in achieving success. In this final chapter, we distill the key takeaways from their experiences and offer practical insights for those looking to make their mark in the world.

One of the most important lessons is the value of a clear and compelling vision. Visionary leaders like Jeff Bezos and Stephen Ross have shown that a strong vision can inspire and guide their organizations, driving them to achieve ambitious goals. A clear vision provides direction, motivates teams, and attracts stakeholders who share the same aspirations. Aspiring leaders should develop a vision that aligns with their values and purpose, and communicate it effectively to their teams.

Innovation is another critical lesson. Tech moguls and real estate tycoons who prioritize innovation are able to stay ahead of the competition and adapt to changing market conditions. This requires a willingness to take risks, experiment, and embrace new ideas. Aspiring leaders should foster a culture of innovation within their organizations, encouraging creativity, collaboration, and continuous learning. By staying curious and open to new possibilities, they can drive progress and achieve breakthroughs.

Resilience is a fundamental trait of successful leaders. The journeys of tech moguls and real estate tycoons are filled with challenges, setbacks, and failures. What sets them apart is their ability to bounce back, learn from their experiences, and persevere in the face of adversity. Aspiring leaders should cultivate resilience by developing a growth mindset, staying adaptable, and maintaining a positive outlook. By viewing challenges as opportunities for growth, they can navigate obstacles and emerge stronger.

Ethical leadership is essential for long-term success. Visionary leaders who prioritize ethical considerations build trust and credibility with their stakeholders. This includes making decisions that are socially responsible, environmentally sustainable, and aligned with their values. Aspiring leaders should uphold high ethical standards, act with integrity, and consider the broader impact of their actions. By doing so, they can create a positive legacy and contribute to a better world.

Finally, continuous learning and personal growth are key to leadership success. Tech moguls and real estate tycoons are lifelong learners who constantly seek to expand their knowledge and skills. Aspiring leaders should invest in their personal and professional development, stay informed about industry trends, and seek mentorship and guidance. By committing to continuous learning, they can stay relevant, innovate, and lead effectively in a rapidly changing world.

Through the stories of tech moguls and real estate tycoons, we gain valuable insights into the principles that drive success. By embracing their lessons and applying them to our own journeys, we can unlock our potential and create a meaningful impact in our respective fields. The future belongs to those who dare to dream, innovate, and lead with vision and purpose.

Visionary Tactics: Comparing the Minds of Tech Moguls and Real Estate Tycoons is an insightful exploration into the worlds of two very different, yet surprisingly similar, industries. The book delves into the strategies, innovation, and leadership styles of both tech leaders and real estate tycoons, highlighting how their visionary approaches have shaped modern commerce. From the dawn of their empires to their strategic vision,

CHAPTER 12: LESSONS FROM VISIONARY LEADERS

financial acumen, and global influence, this book compares and contrasts their journeys, offering valuable lessons for aspiring entrepreneurs and leaders. It also emphasizes the importance of branding, public perception, philanthropy, and social responsibility in building lasting legacies. Through detailed chapters, readers will gain a comprehensive understanding of the principles that drive success in both the tech and real estate industries, and how these visionary leaders continue to inspire and lead the way into the future.

www.ingramcontent.com/pod-product-compliance
Lightning Source LLC
LaVergne TN
LVHW020742090526
838202LV00057BA/6194